# Contents

# Easy Chicken & Biscuits

**Prep Time:** 15 minutes
**Cook Time:** 30 minutes

    **1 can (10¾ ounces) CAMPBELL'S® Cream of Celery Soup or 98% Fat Free Cream of Celery Soup**
    **1 can (10¾ ounces) CAMPBELL'S® Cream of Potato Soup**
    **1 cup milk**
    **¼ teaspoon dried thyme leaves, crushed**
    **¼ teaspoon pepper**
    **4 cups cooked cut-up vegetables***
    **2 cups cubed cooked chicken, turkey or ham**
    **1 package (7½ or 10 ounces) refrigerated buttermilk biscuits (10 biscuits)**

*Use a combination of broccoli flowerets, cauliflower flowerets and sliced carrots or broccoli flowerets and sliced carrots or broccoli flowerets, sliced carrots and peas.*

*1.* In 3-quart shallow baking dish mix soups, milk, thyme, pepper, vegetables and chicken.

*2.* Bake at 400°F. for 15 minutes or until hot.

*3.* Stir. Arrange biscuits over chicken mixture. Bake 15 minutes more or until biscuits are golden.

                 *Makes 5 servings*

**Tip:** To microwave vegetables, in 2-quart shallow microwave-safe baking dish arrange vegetables and ¼ cup water. Cover. Microwave on HIGH 10 minutes.

## CLASSICS

# Chicken Pot Pie

**Prep Time:** 10 minutes
**Cook Time:** 30 minutes

**1 can (10¾ ounces) CAMPBELL'S® Cream of Chicken Soup**
**1 package (about 9 ounces) frozen mixed vegetables, thawed (about 2 cups)**
**1 cup cubed cooked chicken**
**½ cup milk**
**1 egg**
**1 cup all-purpose baking mix**

*1.* Preheat oven to 400°F.

*2.* In 9-inch pie plate mix soup, vegetables and chicken.

*3.* Mix milk, egg and baking mix. Pour over chicken mixture. Bake 30 minutes or until golden.

*Makes 4 servings*

**Turkey Pot Pie:** *Substitute 1 cup cubed cooked turkey for chicken.*

**Tip:** *For a variation, substitute CAMPBELL'S® Condensed Cream of Chicken Soup with Herbs.*

CLASSICS

5

# Honey-Mustard Chicken

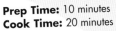

**Prep Time:** 10 minutes
**Cook Time:** 20 minutes

**1 tablespoon butter *or* margarine**
**4 skinless, boneless chicken breast halves**
**(about 1 pound)**
**1 can (10¾ ounces) CAMPBELL'S® Cream of**
**Chicken Soup *or* 98% Fat Free Cream**
**of Chicken Soup**
**¼ cup mayonnaise**
**2 tablespoons honey**
**1 tablespoon spicy brown mustard**
**Chopped toasted pecans *or* walnuts**

*1.* In medium skillet over medium-high heat, heat butter. Add chicken and cook 10 minutes or until browned. Set chicken aside.

*2.* Add soup, mayonnaise, honey and mustard. Heat to a boil. Return chicken to pan. Reduce heat to low. Cover and cook 5 minutes or until chicken is no longer pink.

*3.* Sprinkle with pecans. Serve with rice if desired.
*Makes 4 servings*

**CLASSICS**

6

# Flash Roasted Crispy Ranch Chicken

**Prep Time:** 5 minutes
**Cook Time:** 20 minutes

1 can (10¾ ounces) **CAMPBELL'S® Cream of Chicken Soup** *or* **98% Fat Free Cream of Chicken Soup**
½ cup **milk**
1 envelope (1 ounce) **ranch salad dressing mix**
4 **skinless, boneless chicken breast halves** (about 1 pound)
1½ cups **finely crushed tortilla chips**
2 tablespoons **margarine** *or* **butter, melted**

*1.* In shallow dish mix soup, milk and dressing mix. Reserve 1 cup for sauce.

*2.* Dip chicken into soup mixture. Coat with tortilla chips. Place chicken on greased baking sheet. Drizzle with margarine. Bake at 400°F. for 20 minutes or until chicken is no longer pink.

*3.* In small saucepan over medium heat, heat reserved soup mixture to a boil. Serve with chicken.

*Makes 4 servings*

**CLASSICS**

# Cornbread Chicken Pot Pie

**Prep Time:** 10 minutes
**Cook Time:** 30 minutes

> 1 can (10¾ ounces) **CAMPBELL'S®** Cream of Chicken Soup *or* 98% Fat Free Cream of Chicken Soup
> 1 can (about 8 ounces) whole kernel corn, drained
> 2 cups cubed cooked chicken *or* turkey
> 1 package (8½ ounces) corn muffin mix
> ¾ cup milk
> 1 egg
> ½ cup shredded Cheddar cheese (2 ounces)

*1.* Preheat oven to 400°F. In 9-inch pie plate mix soup, corn and chicken.

*2.* Mix muffin mix, milk and egg. Pour over chicken mixture. Bake for 30 minutes or until golden.

*3.* Sprinkle with cheese. *Makes 4 servings*

***Campbell's® Cornbread Chicken Chili Pot Pie:*** *In Step 1 add 1 can (about 4 ounces) chopped green chilies, drained, with the corn.*

CLASSICS

# Beef Taco Bake

**Prep Time:** 10 minutes
**Cook Time:** 30 minutes

1 pound **ground beef**
1 can (10¾ ounces) **CAMPBELL'S® Condensed Tomato Soup**
1 cup **PACE® Thick & Chunky Salsa** *or* **Picante Sauce**
½ cup **milk**
6 **flour tortillas (8-inch)** *or* 8 **corn tortillas (6-inch), cut into 1-inch pieces**
1 cup **shredded Cheddar cheese (4 ounces)**

*1.* In medium skillet over medium-high heat, cook beef until browned, stirring to separate meat. Pour off fat.

*2.* Add soup, salsa, milk, tortillas and **half** the cheese. Spoon into 2-quart shallow baking dish. **Cover.**

*3.* Bake at 400°F. for 30 minutes or until hot. Sprinkle with remaining cheese.

*Makes 4 servings*

CLASSICS

# Turkey Stuffing Divan

**Prep Time:** 15 minutes
**Cook Time:** 30 minutes

**1¼ cups boiling water**
  **4 tablespoons margarine *or* butter, melted**
  **4 cups PEPPERIDGE FARM® Herb Seasoned Stuffing**
  **2 cups cooked broccoli cuts**
  **2 cups cubed cooked turkey**
  **1 can (10¾ ounces) CAMPBELL'S® Cream of Celery Soup *or* 98% Fat Free Cream of Celery Soup**
**½ cup milk**
  **1 cup shredded Cheddar cheese (4 ounces)**

*1.* Mix water and margarine. Add stuffing. Mix lightly.

*2.* Spoon into 2-quart shallow baking dish. Arrange broccoli and turkey over stuffing. In small bowl mix soup, milk and **½ cup** cheese. Pour over broccoli and turkey. Sprinkle remaining cheese over soup mixture.

*3.* Bake at 350°F. for 30 minutes or until hot.

*Makes 6 servings*

**Variation:** Substitute 1 can (10¾ ounces) CAMPBELL'S® Condensed Cream of Chicken Soup **or** 98% Fat Free Cream of Chicken Soup for Cream of Celery Soup. Substitute 2 cups cubed cooked chicken for turkey.

**Tip:** For 2 cups cooked broccoli cuts use about 1 pound fresh broccoli, trimmed, cut into 1-inch pieces (about 2 cups) **or** 1 package (10 ounces) frozen broccoli cuts (2 cups).

CLASSICS

# Pan Roasted Vegetable & Chicken Pizza

**Prep Time:** 20 minutes
**Cook Time:** 12 minutes

**Vegetable cooking spray**
**¾ pound skinless, boneless chicken breasts, cubed**
**3 cups cut-up vegetables***
**⅛ teaspoon garlic powder**
**1 can (10¾ ounces) CAMPBELL'S® Condensed Cream of Mushroom Soup *or* 98% Fat Free Cream of Mushroom Soup**
**1 Italian bread shell (12-inch)**
**1 cup shredded Monterey Jack cheese (4 ounces)**

*Use a combination of sliced zucchini, red or green pepper cut into 2-inch long strips, and thinly sliced onion.*

*1.* Spray medium skillet with vegetable cooking spray and heat over medium-high heat 1 minute. Add chicken and cook 10 minutes or until browned, stirring often. Set chicken aside.

*2.* Remove pan from heat. Spray with cooking spray. Reduce heat to medium. Add vegetables and garlic powder. Cook until tender-crisp. Add soup. Return chicken to pan. Heat through.

*3.* Spread chicken mixture over shell to within ¼ inch of edge. Top with cheese. Bake at 450°F. for 12 minutes or until cheese is melted.

*Makes 4 servings*

**CLASSICS**

11

# Creamy Pesto Chicken & Bow Ties

**Prep/Cook Time:** 20 minutes

**3 cups** *uncooked* **bow tie pasta**
**2 tablespoons butter** *or* **margarine**
**1 pound skinless, boneless chicken breasts, cubed**
**1 can (10¾ ounces) CAMPBELL'S® Cream of Chicken Soup** *or* **98% Fat Free Cream of Chicken Soup**
**½ cup pesto sauce**
**½ cup milk**

*1.* Cook pasta according to package directions. Drain.

*2.* Meanwhile, heat butter in skillet. Add chicken and cook until browned, stirring often.

*3.* Add soup, pesto sauce and milk. Bring to a boil. Cook over low heat 5 minutes or until done. Stir in drained pasta and heat through.

*Makes 4 servings*

**20 MINUTES**

# Classic Campbelled Eggs

**Prep Time:** 10 minutes
**Cook Time:** 15 minutes

**1 can (10¾ ounces) CAMPBELL'S® Condensed
 Cheddar Cheese Soup
8 eggs, beaten
 Dash pepper
2 tablespoons margarine *or* butter
 Chopped fresh parsley for garnish**

*1.* In medium bowl mix soup, eggs and pepper.

*2.* In medium skillet over low heat, heat margarine.
Add egg mixture. As eggs begin to set, stir lightly so
uncooked egg mixture flows to bottom. Cook until set
but still moist.

*3.* Garnish with parsley.          *Makes 4 servings*

20 MINUTES

# Broccoli Chicken Potato Parmesan

**Prep/Cook Time:** 20 minutes

**2 tablespoons vegetable oil**
**1 pound red potatoes, sliced ¼ inch thick**
**1 package (about 10 ounces) refrigerated cooked chicken strips**
**2 cups fresh *or* frozen broccoli flowerets**
**1 can CAMPBELL'S® Broccoli Cheese Soup *or* 98% Fat Free Broccoli Cheese Soup**
**½ cup milk**
**¼ teaspoon garlic powder**
**¼ cup grated Parmesan cheese**

*1.* Heat oil in skillet. Add potatoes. Cover and cook over medium heat 10 minutes, stirring occasionally.

*2.* Stir in chicken and broccoli.

*3.* Mix soup, milk and garlic. Add to skillet. Sprinkle with cheese. Heat to a boil. Cover and cook over low heat 5 minutes or until done.

*Makes 4 servings*

20 MINUTES

# Beef Taco Skillet

**Prep/Cook Time:** 20 minutes

1 pound ground beef
1 can (10¾ ounces) **CAMPBELL'S®**
   Tomato Soup
1 cup **PACE® Chunky Salsa** *or* **Picante Sauce**
½ cup water
8 flour *or* corn tortillas (6 inches), cut into
   1-inch pieces
1 cup shredded Cheddar cheese

*1.* Cook beef in skillet until browned. Pour off fat.

*2.* Add soup, salsa, water, tortillas and **half** the cheese. Heat to a boil. Cover and cook over low heat 5 minutes or until hot.

*3.* Top with remaining cheese.    *Makes 4 servings*

**20 MINUTES**

15

# Fabulous Fast Shrimp

**Prep/Cook Time:** 20 minutes

   1 tablespoon butter *or* margarine
   2 stalks celery, chopped
   ¼ cup chopped green pepper
   ¼ cup sliced green onions
   1 pound fresh *or* frozen large shrimp,
       shelled and deveined
   1 can (10¾ ounces) CAMPBELL'S® Cream
       of Chicken Soup *or* 98% Fat Free Cream
       of Chicken Soup
   ½ cup water
       Dash of cayenne pepper
       Hot cooked rice
       Paprika

*1.* Heat butter in skillet. Add celery, green pepper and green onions and cook until tender. Add shrimp and cook 3 to 5 minutes or until done.

*2.* Add soup, water and cayenne pepper and heat through.

*3.* Serve over rice. Sprinkle with paprika.

*Makes 4 servings*

20 MINUTES

# Chicken Quesadillas & Fiesta Rice

**Prep/Cook Time:** 20 minutes

**1 pound skinless, boneless chicken breasts,
cubed**
**1 can (10¾ ounces) CAMPBELL'S® Cheddar
Cheese Soup**
**½ cup PACE® Chunky Salsa *or* Picante Sauce
(Medium)**
**10 flour tortillas (8-inch)**
**Campbell's® Fiesta Rice (recipe follows)**

*1.* Preheat oven to 425°F.

*2.* In medium nonstick skillet over medium-high heat,
cook chicken 5 minutes or until no longer pink and
juices evaporate, stirring often. Add soup and salsa.
Heat to a boil, stirring occasionally.

*3.* Place tortillas on 2 baking sheets. Top **half**
of each tortilla with **about ⅓ cup** soup mixture.
Spread to within ½ inch of edge. Moisten edges of
tortilla with water. Fold over and press edges
together. Bake 5 minutes or until hot.

*Makes 4 servings*

***Campbell's® Fiesta Rice:*** *In saucepan heat 1 can
CAMPBELL'S® Condensed Chicken Broth, ½ cup water and
½ cup PACE® Chunky Salsa or Picante Sauce to a boil. Stir
in 2 cups uncooked instant rice. Cover and remove from
heat. Let stand 5 minutes.*

**20 MINUTES**

# Chicken & Broccoli Alfredo

**Prep/Cook Time:** 20 minutes

½ **package** *uncooked* **linguine (8 ounces)**
1 **cup fresh** *or* **frozen broccoli flowerets**
2 **tablespoons butter or margarine**
1 **pound skinless, boneless chicken breasts,
    cubed**
1 **can (10¾ ounces) CAMPBELL'S® Cream of
    Mushroom Soup** *or* **98% Fat Free Cream
    of Mushroom Soup**
½ **cup milk**
½ **cup grated Parmesan cheese**
¼ **teaspoon freshly ground pepper**

*1.* Prepare linguine according to package directions.
Add broccoli for last 4 minutes of cooking time.
Drain.

*2.* In medium skillet over medium-high heat, heat
butter. Add chicken and cook until browned, stirring
often.

*3.* Add soup, milk, cheese, pepper and linguine
mixture and cook through, stirring occasionally.
Serve with additional Parmesan cheese.

*Makes 4 servings*

CHICKEN & PASTA

# Chicken Scampi

**Prep/Cook Time:** 20 minutes

**2 tablespoons butter**
**4 skinless, boneless chicken breast halves**
**(about 1 pound)**
**1 can (10¾ ounces) CAMPBELL'S® Cream of**
**Chicken Soup *or* 98% Fat Free Cream**
**of Chicken Soup**
**¼ cup water**
**2 teaspoons lemon juice**
**2 cloves garlic, minced *or* ¼ teaspoon garlic**
**powder**
**4 cups hot cooked capellini *or* thin spaghetti**

*1.* Heat butter in skillet. Add chicken and cook until browned.

*2.* Add soup, water, lemon juice and garlic. Heat to a boil. Cover and cook over low heat 5 minutes or until done.

*3.* Serve with pasta. *Makes 4 servings*

**CHICKEN & PASTA**

# Shortcut Chicken Cordon Bleu

**Prep Time:** 10 minutes
**Cook Time:** 20 minutes

- 1 tablespoon margarine *or* butter
- 4 skinless, boneless chicken breast halves (about 1 pound)
- 1 can (10¾ ounces) CAMPBELL'S® Cream of Chicken Soup *or* 98% Fat Free Cream of Chicken Soup
- 2 tablespoons water
- 2 tablespoons Chablis *or* other dry white wine
- ½ cup shredded Swiss cheese (2 ounces)
- ½ cup chopped cooked ham
- 4 cups hot cooked medium egg noodles (about 3 cups uncooked)

*1.* In medium skillet over medium-high heat, heat margarine. Add chicken and cook 10 minutes or until browned. Set chicken aside.

*2.* Add soup, water, wine, cheese and ham. Heat to a boil, stirring often. Return chicken to pan.

*3.* Reduce heat to low. Cover and cook 5 minutes or until chicken is no longer pink, stirring occasionally. Serve with noodles.      *Makes 4 servings*

**Tip:** *Store uncooked chicken in the coldest part of your refrigerator for no more than 2 days before cooking.*

CHICKEN & PASTA

# Chicken Asparagus Gratin

**Prep Time:** 20 minutes
**Cook Time:** 30 minutes

  1 can (10¾ ounces) **CAMPBELL'S®** Cream of
        **Asparagus Soup**
  ½ cup milk
  ¼ teaspoon onion powder
  ⅛ teaspoon pepper
  3 cups hot cooked corkscrew macaroni
        (about 2½ cups uncooked)
1½ cups cubed cooked chicken *or* turkey
1½ cups cooked cut asparagus
  1 cup shredded Cheddar *or* Swiss cheese
        (4 ounces)

*1.* In 2-quart casserole mix soup, milk, onion
powder and pepper. Stir in macaroni, chicken,
asparagus and ½ **cup** cheese.

*2.* Bake at 400°F. for 25 minutes or until hot.

*3.* Stir. Sprinkle remaining cheese over chicken
mixture. Bake 5 minutes more or until cheese is
melted.                               *Makes 4 servings*

**Tip:** *For 1½ cups cooked cut asparagus, cook ¾ pound
fresh asparagus, trimmed and cut into 1-inch pieces, or
1 package (about 9 ounces) frozen asparagus cuts.*

CHICKEN & PASTA

# Healthy Request®
# Chicken Mozzarella

**Prep Time:** 10 minutes
**Cook Time:** 20 minutes

> **4 skinless, boneless chicken breast halves (about 1 pound)**
> **1 can (10¾ ounces) CAMPBELL'S® HEALTHY REQUEST® Tomato Soup**
> **½ teaspoon Italian seasoning *or* dried oregano leaves, crushed**
> **½ teaspoon garlic powder**
> **¼ cup shredded mozzarella cheese (1 ounce)**
> **4 cups hot cooked corkscrew macaroni (about 3 cups uncooked), cooked without salt**

*1.* Place chicken in 2-quart shallow baking dish.

*2.* Mix soup, Italian seasoning and garlic powder. Spoon over chicken and bake at 400°F. for 20 minutes or until chicken is no longer pink.

*3.* Sprinkle cheese over chicken. Remove chicken. Stir sauce. Serve with macaroni.

*Makes 4 servings*

**CHICKEN & PASTA**

# Tomato-Basil Chicken

**Prep Time:** 5 minutes
**Cook Time:** 20 minutes

- **1 tablespoon vegetable oil**
- **4 skinless, boneless breast halves (about 1 pound)**
- **1 can (10¾ ounces) CAMPBELL'S® Tomato Soup**
- **½ cup milk**
- **2 tablespoons grated Parmesan cheese**
- **½ teaspoon dried basil leaves, crushed**
- **¼ teaspoon garlic powder *or* 2 cloves garlic, minced**
- **4 cups hot cooked medium tube-shaped macaroni (about 3 cups uncooked)**

*1.* In medium skillet over medium-high heat, heat oil. Add chicken and cook 10 minutes or until browned. Set chicken aside. Pour off fat.

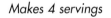

*2.* Add soup, milk, cheese, basil and garlic powder. Heat to a boil. Return chicken to pan. Reduce heat to low. Cover and cook 5 minutes or until chicken is no longer pink.

*3.* Serve with macaroni.              *Makes 4 servings*

**CHICKEN & PASTA**

# Asian Chicken & Rice Bake

**Prep Time:** 5 minutes
**Cook Time:** 45 minutes

- **¾ cup *uncooked* regular white rice**
- **4 skinless, boneless chicken breast halves (about 1 pound)**
- **1 can (10¾ ounces) CAMPBELL'S® Golden Mushroom Soup**
- **¾ cup water**
- **2 tablespoons soy sauce**
- **2 tablespoons cider vinegar**
- **2 tablespoons honey**
- **1 teaspoon garlic powder**
  **Paprika**

*1.* Spread rice in 2-quart shallow baking dish. Place chicken on rice.

*2.* Mix soup, water, soy sauce, vinegar, honey and garlic powder. Pour over chicken. Sprinkle with paprika. **Cover.**

*3.* Bake at 375°F. for 45 minutes or until chicken is no longer pink and rice is done.

*Makes 4 servings*

***Campbell's® Sesame Asian Chicken & Rice Bake:*** *Sprinkle with toasted sesame seeds after baking.*

CHICKEN & RICE

# Fiesta Chicken & Rice Bake

**Prep Time:** 5 minutes
**Cook Time:** 45 minutes

1 can (10¾ ounces) **CAMPBELL'S**® Cream of
    Chicken Soup *or* 98% Fat Free Cream
    of Chicken Soup
1 cup **PACE**® Chunky Salsa *or* Picante Sauce
½ cup water
1 cup whole kernel corn
¾ cup *uncooked* regular white rice
4 skinless, boneless chicken breast halves
    (about 1 pound)
    Paprika
½ cup shredded Cheddar cheese (2 ounces)

*1.* In 2-quart shallow baking dish mix soup, salsa,
water, corn and rice. Place chicken on rice mixture.
Sprinkle paprika over chicken. **Cover.**

*2.* Bake at 375°F. for 45 minutes or until chicken is
no longer pink and rice is done.

*3.* Sprinkle with cheese.     *Makes 4 servings*

CHICKEN & RICE

# Chicken & Roasted Garlic Risotto

**Prep/Cook Time:** 20 minutes

**4 skinless, boneless chicken breast halves
(about 1 pound)**
**1 tablespoon butter *or* margarine**
**1 can (10¾ ounces) CAMPBELL'S® Cream
of Chicken Soup *or* 98% Fat Free Cream
of Chicken Soup**
**1 can CAMPBELL'S® Cream of Mushroom
with Roasted Garlic Soup**
**2 cups water**
**2 cups *uncooked* instant rice**
**1 cup frozen peas and carrots**

*1.* Season chicken.

*2.* Heat butter in skillet. Add chicken and cook
10 minutes or until browned. Remove chicken.

*3.* Add soups and water. Heat to a boil. Stir in rice
and vegetables. Top with chicken. Cover and cook
over low heat 5 minutes or until done. Remove from
heat. Let stand 5 minutes.            *Makes 4 servings*

CHICKEN & RICE

# Skillet Fiesta Chicken & Rice

**Prep Time:** 5 minutes
**Cook Time:** 20 minutes

- 1 tablespoon vegetable oil
- 4 skinless, boneless chicken breast halves (about 1 pound)
- 1 can (10¾ ounces) CAMPBELL'S® Tomato Soup

- 1⅓ cups water
- 1 teaspoon chili powder
- 1½ cups *uncooked* instant rice
- ¼ cup shredded Cheddar cheese (1 ounce)

*1.* In medium skillet over medium-high heat, heat oil. Add chicken and cook 10 minutes or until browned. Set chicken aside. Pour off fat.

*2.* Add soup, water and chili powder. Heat to a boil.

*3.* Stir in rice. Place chicken on rice mixture. Sprinkle chicken with additional chili powder and cheese. Reduce heat to low. Cover and cook 5 minutes or until chicken and rice are done. Stir rice mixture.

*Makes 4 servings*

CHICKEN & RICE

# Homestyle Beef Stew

**Prep Time:** 10 minutes
**Cook Time:** 2 hours 15 minutes

- **2 tablespoons all-purpose flour**
- **⅛ teaspoon pepper**
- **1 pound beef for stew, cut into 1-inch cubes**
- **1 tablespoon vegetable oil**
- **1 can (10½ ounces) CAMPBELL'S® Beef Broth**
- **½ cup water**
- **½ teaspoon dried thyme leaves, crushed**
- **1 bay leaf**
- **3 medium carrots (about ½ pound), cut into 1-inch pieces**
- **2 medium potatoes (about ½ pound), cut into quarters**

*1.* Mix flour and pepper. Coat beef with flour mixture. In large heavy pot over medium-high heat, heat oil. Add beef and cook until browned, stirring often. Set beef aside. Pour off fat.

*2.* Add broth, water, thyme and bay leaf. Heat to a boil. Return beef to pan. Reduce heat to low. Cover and cook 1½ hours.

*3.* Add carrots and potatoes. Cover and cook 30 minutes or until beef is fork-tender, stirring occasionally. Discard bay leaf.

*Makes 4 servings*

**BEEF**

# Simply Delicious Meat Loaf

**Prep Time:** 5 minutes
**Cook Time:** 1 hour 5 minutes

1½ **pounds ground beef**
½ **cup Italian-seasoned dry bread crumbs**
1 **egg, beaten**
1 **can (10¾ ounces) CAMPBELL'S® Golden Mushroom Soup**
¼ **cup water**

*1.* Mix beef, bread crumbs and egg **thoroughly.** In medium baking pan shape firmly into 8×4-inch loaf.

*2.* Bake at 350°F. for 30 minutes. Spread ½ **can** soup over top of meat loaf. Bake 30 minutes more or until meat loaf is no longer pink (160°F.).

*3.* In small saucepan mix **2 tablespoons** drippings, remaining soup and water. Heat through. Serve with meat loaf.          *Makes 6 servings*

BEEF

# Garlic Mashed Potatoes & Beef Bake

**Prep Time:** 10 minutes
**Cook Time:** 20 minutes

- **1 pound ground beef**
- **1 can (10¾ ounces) CAMPBELL'S® Cream of Mushroom with Roasted Garlic Soup**
- **1 tablespoon Worcestershire sauce**
- **1 bag (16 ounces) frozen vegetable combination (broccoli, cauliflower, carrots), thawed**
- **3 cups hot mashed potatoes**

*1.* In medium skillet over medium-high heat, cook beef until browned, stirring to separate meat. Pour off fat.

*2.* In 2-quart shallow baking dish mix beef, ½ **can** soup, Worcestershire and vegetables.

*3.* Stir remaining soup into potatoes. Spoon potato mixture over beef mixture. Bake at 400°F. for 20 minutes or until hot.          *Makes 4 servings*

BEEF

# Country Beef & Vegetables

**Prep Time:** 5 minutes
**Cook Time:** 20 minutes

1½ **pounds ground beef**
1 **can (26 ounces) CAMPBELL'S® Tomato Soup**
1 **tablespoon Worcestershire sauce**
1 **bag (16 ounces) frozen mixed vegetables**
6 **cups hot cooked rice**
  **Shredded Cheddar cheese**

*1.* In medium skillet over medium-high heat, cook beef until browned, stirring to separate meat. Pour off fat.

*2.* Add soup, Worcestershire and vegetables. Heat to a boil. Reduce heat to low. Cook 5 minutes or until vegetables are tender.

*3.* Serve over rice. Top with cheese.

*Makes 6 servings*

BEEF

# Easy Beef Teriyaki

**Prep Time:** 10 minutes
**Cook Time:** 20 minutes

1 pound boneless beef sirloin steak,
  ¾ inch thick
1 tablespoon vegetable oil
1 can (10¾ ounces) **CAMPBELL'S®** Golden
  Mushroom Soup
2 tablespoons soy sauce
1 tablespoon packed brown sugar
1 bag (about 16 ounces) frozen Oriental
  stir-fry vegetables
4 cups hot cooked rice

*1.* Slice beef into very thin strips.

*2.* In medium skillet over medium-high heat, heat oil. Add beef and stir-fry until beef is browned and juices evaporate.

*3.* Add soup, soy sauce and sugar. Heat to a boil. Reduce heat to medium. Add vegetables. Cover and cook 5 minutes until vegetables are tender-crisp, stirring occasionally. Serve over rice.

*Makes 4 servings*

**BEEF**

# Spicy Salsa Mac & Beef

**Prep Time:** 5 minutes
**Cook Time:** 25 minutes

   **1 pound ground beef**
   **1 can (10½ ounces) CAMPBELL'S® Beef Broth**
**1⅓ cups water**
   **2 cups *uncooked* medium shell or elbow**
       **macaroni**
   **1 can (10¾ ounces) CAMPBELL'S® Cheddar**
       **Cheese Soup**
   **1 cup PACE® Chunky Salsa**

*1.* In medium skillet over medium-high heat, cook beef until browned, stirring to separate meat. Pour off fat.

*2.* Add broth and water. Heat to a boil. Stir in macaroni. Reduce heat to medium. Cook 10 minutes or until macaroni is done, stirring often.

*3.* Stir in soup and salsa and heat through.

*Makes 4 servings*

BEEF

# Polynesian Pork Chops

**Prep/Cook Time:** 20 minutes

4 boneless pork chops, ¾ inch thick
1 teaspoon garlic powder
1 tablespoon vegetable oil
1 medium onion, chopped
1 can **CAMPBELL'S®** Golden Mushroom Soup
1 can (8 ounces) pineapple chunks
¼ cup water
3 tablespoons soy sauce
1 tablespoon honey
2 cups cooked instant rice
Sliced green onions

*1.* Season chops with garlic. Heat oil in skillet. Add chops and cook until browned. Add onion.

*2.* Add soup, pineapple with juice, water, soy and honey. Heat to a boil. Cook over low heat 10 minutes or until done.

*3.* Serve with rice and garnish with green onions.
*Makes 4 servings*

PORK

# Mushroom Garlic Pork Chops

**Prep Time:** 5 minutes
**Cook Time:** 20 minutes

**1 tablespoon vegetable oil**
**4 pork chops, ½ inch thick (about 1 pound)**
**1 can (10¾ ounces) CAMPBELL'S® Cream of**
    **Mushroom with Roasted Garlic Soup**
**¼ cup water**

*1.* In medium skillet over medium-high heat, heat oil. Add chops and cook 10 minutes or until browned. Set chops aside. Pour off fat.

*2.* Add soup and water. Heat to a boil.

*3.* Return chops to pan. Reduce heat to low. Cover and cook 5 minutes or until chops are no longer pink. *Makes 4 servings*

PORK

# Cajun Fish

**Prep Time:** 10 minutes
**Cook Time:** 15 minutes

- 1 tablespoon vegetable oil
- 1 small green pepper, diced (about ⅔ cup)
- ½ teaspoon dried oregano leaves, crushed
- 1 can (10¾ ounces) CAMPBELL'S® Tomato Soup
- ⅓ cup water
- ⅛ teaspoon garlic powder
- ⅛ teaspoon black pepper
- ⅛ teaspoon ground red pepper
- 1 pound firm white fish fillets (cod, haddock or halibut)

*1.* In medium skillet over medium heat, heat oil. Add green pepper and oregano and cook until tender-crisp, stirring often.

*2.* Add soup, water, garlic powder, black pepper and red pepper. Heat to a boil.

*3.* Place fish in soup mixture. Reduce heat to low. Cover and cook 5 minutes or until fish flakes easily when tested with a fork. Serve with rice if desired.

*Makes 4 servings*

**FISH**

# Healthy Request®
# Primavera Fish Fillets

**Prep Time:** 10 minutes
**Cook Time:** 20 minutes

 1 **large carrot, cut into matchstick-thin strips**
  **(about 1 cup)**
 2 **stalks celery, cut into matchstick-thin strips**
  **(about 1 cup)**
 1 **small onion, diced (about ¼ cup)**
 ¼ **cup water**
 2 **tablespoons Chablis** *or* **other dry**
  **white wine**
 ½ **teaspoon dried thyme leaves, crushed**
  **Generous dash pepper**
 1 **can (10¾ ounces) CAMPBELL'S® HEALTHY**
  **REQUEST® Cream of Mushroom Soup**
 1 **pound firm white fish fillets (cod, haddock**
  **or halibut)**

*1.* In medium skillet mix carrot, celery, onion, water, wine, thyme and pepper. Over medium-high heat, heat to a boil. Reduce heat to low. Cover and cook 5 minutes or until vegetables are tender-crisp.

*2.* Stir in soup. Over medium heat, heat to a boil.

*3.* Place fish in soup mixture. Reduce heat to low. Cover and cook 5 minutes or until fish flakes easily when tested with a fork.   *Makes 4 servings*

FISH

# Florentine Casserole

**Prep Time:** 10 minutes
**Cook Time:** 35 minutes

> **4 cups PEPPERIDGE FARM® Herb Seasoned Stuffing**
> **1 tablespoon margarine *or* butter, melted**
> **1 can (10¾ ounces) CAMPBELL'S® Cream of Celery Soup *or* 98% Fat Free Cream of Celery Soup**
> **½ cup sour cream *or* plain yogurt**
> **1 teaspoon onion powder**
> **1 package (about 10 ounces) frozen chopped spinach, thawed**
> **¼ cup grated Parmesan cheese**

*1.* Mix ½ **cup** stuffing and margarine. Set aside.

*2.* Mix soup, sour cream, onion powder, spinach and cheese. Add remaining stuffing. Mix lightly. Spoon into 1½-quart casserole. Sprinkle reserved stuffing mixture over top.

*3.* Bake at 350°F. for 35 minutes or until hot.

*Makes 6 servings*

**Tip:** To thaw spinach, microwave on HIGH 3 minutes, breaking apart with fork halfway through heating.

# One-Dish Pasta & Vegetables

**Prep Time:** 15 minutes
**Cook Time:** 15 minutes

1½ **cups** *uncooked* **corkscrew macaroni**
  2 **medium carrots, sliced (about 1 cup)**
  1 **cup broccoli flowerets**
  1 **can (10¾ ounces) CAMPBELL'S® Cheddar**
    **Cheese Soup**
½ **cup milk**
  1 **tablespoon prepared mustard**

*1.* In large saucepan prepare macaroni according to package directions.

*2.* Add carrots and broccoli for last 5 minutes of cooking time. Drain.

*3.* In same pan mix soup, milk, mustard and macaroni mixture. Over medium heat, heat through, stirring often. *Makes 5 servings*

VEGETABLES

# Quick Beef 'n' Beans Tacos

**Prep Time:** 15 minutes
**Cook Time:** 10 minutes

- **1 pound ground beef**
- **1 small onion, chopped (about ¼ cup)**
- **1 can (11¼ ounces) CAMPBELL'S® Fiesta Chili Beef Soup**
- **¼ cup water**
- **10 taco shells**
  - **Shredded Cheddar cheese, shredded lettuce, diced tomato and sour cream**

*1.* In medium skillet over medium-high heat, cook beef and onion until beef is browned, stirring to separate meat. Pour off fat.

*2.* Add soup and water. Reduce heat to low. Cover and cook 5 minutes.

*3.* Divide meat mixture among taco shells. Top with cheese, lettuce, tomato and sour cream.

*Makes 10 tacos*

**TACOS**

# Beef & Cheddar Soft Tacos

**Prep/Cook Time:** 15 minutes

- **1 pound ground beef**
- **1 can (10¾ ounces) CAMPBELL'S® Cheddar Cheese Soup**
- **½ cup PACE® Chunky Salsa *or* Picante Sauce**
- **8 flour tortillas (8-inch)**
- **2 cups shredded lettuce (about ½ small head)**

*1.* In medium skillet over medium-high heat, cook beef until browned, stirring to separate meat. Pour off fat.

*2.* Add soup and salsa. Reduce heat to low and heat through.

*3.* Spoon **about ⅓ cup** meat mixture down center of each tortilla. Top with lettuce. Fold tortilla around filling. Serve with additional salsa.

*Makes 4 servings*

TACOS

# Buffalo-Style Burgers

**Prep/Cook Time:** 20 minutes

> **1 pound ground beef**
> **1 can (10¾ ounces) CAMPBELL'S®**
>   **Tomato Soup**
> **⅛ teaspoon hot pepper sauce**
> **4 hamburger rolls, split and toasted**
> **½ cup crumbled blue cheese (about**
>   **4 ounces)**

*1.* Shape beef into 4 patties, ½ inch thick. In medium skillet over medium-high heat, cook patties until browned. Set patties aside. Pour off fat.

*2.* Add soup and hot pepper sauce. Heat to a boil. Return patties to pan. Reduce heat to low. Cover and cook 10 minutes or until patties are no longer pink (160°F.).

*3.* Place patties on 4 roll halves. Top with cheese and remaining roll halves. *Makes 4 sandwiches*

BURGERS

# French Onion Burgers

**Prep/Cook Time:** 20 minutes

- **1 pound ground beef**
- **1 can (10½ ounces) CAMPBELL'S® French Onion Soup**
- **4 round hard rolls, split**
- **4 slices cheese (use your favorite)**

*1.* Shape beef into 4 patties, ½ inch thick. In medium skillet over medium-high heat, cook patties until browned. Set patties aside. Pour off fat.

*2.* Add soup. Heat to a boil. Return patties to pan. Reduce heat to low. Cover and cook 10 minutes or until patties are no longer pink (160°F.).

*3.* Place cheese on patties and cook until cheese is melted. Place patties on 4 roll halves. Serve with soup mixture for dipping.　　　*Makes 4 sandwiches*

# Southwestern Chicken & Pepper Wraps

**Prep Time:** 10 minutes
**Cook/Stand Time:** 25 minutes

2 tablespoons vegetable oil
1 pound skinless, boneless chicken breasts,
   cut into strips
1 medium red pepper, cut into 2-inch long
   strips (about 1½ cups)
1 medium green pepper, cut into 2-inch long
   strips (about 1½ cups)
1 small onion, sliced (about ¼ cup)
1 can (10¾ ounces) CAMPBELL'S® Golden
   Mushroom Soup
1 cup water
1 cup black beans, rinsed and drained
   (optional)
1 cup *uncooked* instant rice
8 flour tortillas (8-inch)

*1.* In medium skillet over medium-high heat, heat **half** the oil. Add chicken and cook 10 minutes or until no longer pink and juices evaporate, stirring often.

*2.* Reduce heat to medium. Add remaining oil. Add peppers and onion and cook until tender-crisp, stirring often. Add soup, water and beans. Heat to a boil. Stir in rice. Cover and remove from heat. Let stand 5 minutes.

*3.* Spoon **¾ cup** chicken mixture down center of each tortilla. Fold tortilla around filling.

*Makes 4 servings*

SANDWICHES

# Quick Tangy Roast Beef Sandwiches

**Prep/Cook Time:** 15 minutes

**1 can (10¾ ounces) CAMPBELL'S®
   Tomato Soup**
**2 tablespoons vinegar**
**1 tablespoon packed brown sugar**
**1 tablespoon Worcestershire sauce**
**12 ounces sliced cooked deli beef**
**4 hamburger rolls**

*1.* Mix soup, vinegar, sugar and Worcestershire in skillet. Heat to a boil.

*2.* Add beef and heat through.

*3.* Serve on rolls.     *Makes 4 sandwiches*

**SANDWICHES**

45

# Ham & Broccoli Shortcut Stromboli

**Prep Time:** 10 minutes
**Cook Time:** 20 minutes

1 package (10 ounces) refrigerated pizza
    dough
1 can (10¾ ounces) CAMPBELL'S® Cream of
    Celery Soup
1 cup cooked chopped broccoli
2 cups cubed cooked ham
1 cup shredded Cheddar cheese (4 ounces)

*1.* Preheat oven to 400°F. Unroll dough onto greased baking sheet. Set aside.

*2.* Mix soup, broccoli and ham. Spread soup mixture down center of dough. Top with cheese. Fold long sides of dough over filling and pinch to seal. Pinch short sides to seal.

*3.* Bake 20 minutes or until golden brown. Slice and serve.                    *Makes 4 servings*

***Campbell's® Roast Beef & Bean Shortcut Stromboli:*** *Substitute 1 can CAMPBELL'S® Condensed Cream of Mushroom Soup, 1 cup cut green beans and 2 cups cubed cooked roast beef for Cream of Celery Soup, broccoli and ham.*

***Campbell's® Chicken & Vegetable Shortcut Stromboli:*** *Substitute 1 can CAMPBELL'S® Condensed Cream of Chicken Soup, 1 cup mixed vegetables and 2 cups cubed cooked chicken **or** turkey for Cream of Celery Soup, broccoli and ham.*

**SANDWICHES**